W9-BLL-559

FIRST AMERICANS

The Pueblo

MARIAN BROIDA

 **Marshall Cavendish**
Benchmark
New York

ACKNOWLEDGMENTS

Series consultant: Raymond Bial

The author wishes to thank Christine Abeita of San Felipe Pueblo; Leland Dennis,
Hopi Community Scholar for the Mural Project and Heritage Program Community Liaison,
Museum of Northern Arizona, Flagstaff; and April and Mae Tapia of Santa Clara Pueblo.

Marshall Cavendish Benchmark
99 White Plains Road
Tarrytown, New York 10591-9001
www.marshallcavendish.us

Text copyright © 2006 by Marshall Cavendish Corporation
Map copyright © 2006 by Marshall Cavendish Corporation
Map by Christopher Santoro

Library of Congress Cataloging-in-Publication Data
Broida, Marian.
  The Pueblo / by Marian Broida.
    p. cm. -- (First Americans)
  Includes bibliographical references and index.
  ISBN 0-7614-1898-9
  1. Pueblo Indians--History--Juvenile literature. 2. Pueblo
Indians--Social life and customs--Juvenile literature. I. Title II.
Series: Broida, Marian. First Americans.

  E99.P9B746 2005
  978.9004'974--dc22

                    2004022299

Series design by Symon Chow

Printed in China
1 3 5 6 4 2

Cover: A young girl dressed for her role in a corn dance at Santa Clara Pueblo in New Mexico.
Title page: A pueblo in Taos, New Mexico

Photo Research by Joan Meisel
Cover Photo: Farrell Grehan/Corbis

The photographs in this book are used by permission and through the courtesy of:
AP/Wide World Photos: 39; *Bruce Coleman, Inc.*: Bob Burch, 14; M. Timothy O'Keefe, 30. *Corbis*: Lester Lefkowitz, 16; Horace Bristol, 18; Adam Woolfitt, 22, 40; AINACO, 26; David Muench, 27; Craig Aurness, 32; Buddy Mays, 35; Chris Rainier, 38. *Envision*: Steven Needham, 20. *Getty Images*: David Frazier, 34. *North Wind Picture Archives*: 4, 6-7, 10, 12, 17. *Photo Researchers, Inc.*: Chester Higgins, Jr., 1; Tim Davis, 8; Lawrence Migdale, 19; Russell D. Curtis, 28; Porterfield/Chickering, 36. The Philbrook Museum of Art, Tulsa, Oklahoma: *Blessing of the Deer Dancer*, 1964. Gilbert Benjamin Atencio, San Ildefonso, (1930-1995). Casein and watercolor on paper. Museum purchase 1964, 24.

CONTENTS

1 · WHO ARE THE PUEBLO PEOPLE?

For over fifteen thousand years **Pueblo Indians** have made their home on the dry land of the American Southwest. Gray-green bushes dot the landscape and cliffs rise steeply into a vivid blue sky. Bright sun shines on the sandy soil. In winter, snow falls in the mountains, cloaking the pine and juniper trees. Rattlesnakes, rabbits, and lizards share this spectacular land.

Pueblo Indians are not one tribe, but many. The word **pueblo** comes from the Spanish word for village. There are nineteen independent pueblos in New Mexico, each the home of a different tribe. Most of these border the Rio Grande River, while three pueblos—Laguna, Acoma, and Zuni—are in drier lands. The Hopi live in the Arizona desert, in pueblos on flat-topped hills called **mesas.**

The Pueblo have been performing ceremonial dances for centuries.

The Pueblo Creation Story

Each pueblo has its own story of creation. In all the stories, people first lived underground. **Sacred** beings guided them upward until they reached the earth's surface. After emerging, the people wandered until they found their true

home. The Zunis call this home "the middle place." In their story, the leaders asked an enormous sacred insect, a water strider, to stretch out its arms and legs. They found the middle place by looking under its heart.

Some time between 38,000 and 12,000 years ago, ancestors of today's American Indians walked across a bridge of ice that connected Asia to America. As they spread across North America, some settled in the Southwest. In time, southwestern Indians began to make baskets, grow corn, and build homes called **pit houses** that were partly underground. These people included the first Pueblo Indians.

The remains of an Anasazi, or Pueblo ancestor, village.

This map shows present-day pueblos of New Mexico, located near the Rio Grande, and the Hopi pueblos in Arizona.

Between the years 1050 and 1300 C.E., the Pueblos developed a great civilization. Their homes included spectacular apartment buildings with dozens of rooms, built on mountaintops or under cliffs. They made fine pottery, wove cotton, fashioned stunning **turquoise** jewelry, and built hundreds of miles of roads between their cities. The Navajo name for these people is **Anasazi**. Some people prefer to call them Pueblo ancestors.

The Pueblo started building villages like this one in Taos, New Mexico about 700 years ago.

About the year 1300, something—perhaps drought—forced the Pueblos from their mountain cities. Many settled in smaller pueblos by the Rio Grande River or in the desert. Spanish explorers arrived in the 1500s, bringing terrible times to the peaceful Pueblos. Claiming the region for their king, the Spanish took the Pueblos' food and forced the Indians to work for them. Missionaries tried to make the Pueblos adopt the Catholic religion. Whole villages were abandoned as many Pueblos fled or died as a result of violence, starvation, or disease.

In 1680 the Pueblos revolted and drove the Spaniards out. When the Spanish returned a dozen years later, they treated the Pueblos less cruelly. The Pueblos began adopting some Spanish customs. Most became Catholics but continued to practice their own religion in secret.

In 1821 the Spanish colony of Mexico—which included the Southwest—declared independence from Spain. Twenty-seven years later, Mexico signed a **treaty** giving the Southwest

Spanish explorers arriving in the 1500s often killed Pueblos who did not give them food, clothing, and shelter.

Territory to the United States. The Pueblos became U.S. citizens, with rights to their village lands. However, American settlers claimed much of the land that Pueblos used for grazing animals and farming. Many Pueblos had to find new ways to do things in order to survive.

Today, the Pueblo people continue to thrive. Their rich **heritage** combines ancient Pueblo traditions with customs from Spain, Mexico, and the United States.

2 · LIFE IN THE DESERT

Pueblos have been farmers for at least fifteen hundred years. To raise crops in such dry land, they paid attention to everything around them: wind, water, clouds, the seasons. Corn has long been their most sacred and important food. Before the Spanish came, the Pueblos also grew squash, beans, and pumpkins and collected wild foods such as sunflower seeds. The Spanish taught them to raise sheep and cattle and to grow wheat, melons, and other crops.

Traditional Pueblo homes came from the earth. Many were built from sandstone held in place with mud. Eastern pueblos were often made from **adobe**—clay mixed with straw, dried in the sun, and formed into bricks.

Acoma Pueblo, also known as Sky City, was built on top of a 367-foot sandstone mesa. This location kept the people safe from their enemies.

The earliest pueblos were single dwellings stacked on top of one another, forming villages. Ladders allowed people to climb from level to level. Flat roofs of some lower homes became yards for the homes above them. Most early pueblos had an entrance in the roof. Ladders could be pulled up at night for protection.

Taos Pueblo in New Mexico looks much the same today as it did when the first Spanish explorers arrived in 1540.

Today, a few pueblos, such as Taos, still have homes stacked one above another in the traditional way. In other villages each house is a separate building.

Pueblo life has changed in the last century. Once, men from related families worked together, farming the same plots of land. In some pueblos the men traveled north each year to hunt buffalo. Women and girls spent hours each day grinding corn on grindstones called **metates**. They shaped pottery, cooked, and tended gardens.

Pueblo women making pottery sometime in the 1800s. The Pueblos are still known for their fine pottery.

17

Maria Martinez

Maria Martinez of San Ildefonso Pueblo became famous for her elegant black pottery. In 1919 she and her husband, Julian, developed a way to make pottery following ancient traditions. After Julian's death, Maria continued her work with other family members. She won many awards before she died in 1980.

Boys learned from their male relatives, and girls from their mothers, grand-mothers, and aunts.

Everything people did was part of their religion. For example, before digging clay from the earth, women thanked Clay Old Woman, a sacred being.

While much of Pueblo culture has changed, the heart of it remains the same. Families enjoy traditional foods, such as cornmeal dumplings, paper-thin bread called **piki**, and fragrant loaves of wheat bread baked in outdoor ovens. They cook

Bread is baked in the traditional way at Cochiti Pueblo in New Mexico.

Pueblo Bread Pudding

This dessert is enjoyed in many different pueblos. Each family has its favorite way to make it.

Ingredients:

- 6 slices raisin bread
- 4 thin slices mild cheddar or American cheese
- 1 cup pancake syrup
- 1 cup warm water

1. Ask an adult to help.
2. Preheat the oven to 350°F (176°C).
3. Toast the bread.
4. Lay two slices of toast side by side in a loaf pan. (If they don't fit, trim them.)
5. Place a slice of cheese on each piece of toast.
6. Add two more toast slices, and top with the remaining cheese.
7. Add the last slices of toast.
8. Mix the syrup and water in a bowl, then pour it on top.
9. Cover the pan with foil. Use pot holders to put it in the oven. Bake for 15 minutes.
10. Use pot holders to take out the pan. Let it cool a few minutes. Serve topped with ice cream or cinnamon.

A group of dancers in traditional dress.

stews from meat, chili peppers, and beans, using beef instead of the deer meat their ancestors ate.

Today, most Pueblos wear modern American clothing. But on feast days they often dress as their ancestors did. Men dancing in sacred **rituals** wear white **kilts**, leggings, moccasins, and woven belts. Women and girls wear **mantas**—sleeveless dresses covering one shoulder—along with colorful shawls and sometimes knee-high white moccasins.

More than most Americans, the Pueblos see themselves as part of the natural world. Their community includes not only people but also animals, plants, mountains and lakes, lightning and clouds. They honor the earth for providing everything they need.

To the Pueblos everything in nature is sacred. They see spirits in the world around them—even in clay pots, woven cloth, and houses. Everything has its own life spirit. Corn is especially holy because without it the Pueblo people would not have survived. Many Pueblo rituals include corn.

Each pueblo has its own feast days with daylong dances in the **plaza**. Like their ancestors, Pueblos dance to help the rain to fall and the crops to grow and to help keep the world

This painting by Gilbert Atencio is called *Blessing of the Deer Dancer*. The Deer Dance is part of one of the many celebrations the Pueblo hold throughout the year to honor the world around them.

This pottery sculpture of Corn Mother was made by Joe Cajero, Jr. of Jemez Pueblo. Corn Mother, one of the most important figures in Pueblo mythology, represents growth and life.

in balance. In long lines, moving to the beat of drums, Pueblos of all ages dance as a form of prayer.

Pueblo rituals mark important times in a person's life, such as birth, becoming a teenager, marriage, and death. Among the Hopis, babies are introduced to the sun at a few days of age and blessed with a perfect ear of corn. At about twelve years old, Hopi girls grind corn for four days, hidden behind a curtain. A Hopi groom gives his bride two blankets: one to wear at the wedding ceremony and one for her body to be wrapped in when she dies.

Before a dance, dancers prepare in a **kiva**–a special room for religious ceremonies. Every pueblo contains at least one. Kivas come from the time of the Pueblo ancestors. They are modeled on the pit houses used by the earliest Pueblos.

The inside of a kiva, the underground room where secret ceremonies take place. Even today, outsiders are not allowed to enter these holy places.

The Deer Dance

It is February in Santa Clara Pueblo. Men wearing antlers and white kilts line up in the plaza for the Deer Dance. At the sound of a gun they scatter, chased by the women. Catching one of these "deer" is an honor.

April Tapia, a fifth-grader from Santa Clara, caught a little deer at one Deer Dance. "The little boys dance the Deer Dance separate from the big ones, so the little ones don't get hurt," she explains. "When you catch a deer, you take him home and feed him. Then you send him to his house with a basket of fruits and vegetables."

April has been dancing at ceremonies since she was seven. "I am learning my heritage," she says.

Most Pueblo Indians practice both Catholic and Pueblo religions. Saint Francis Church (above) at Ranchos de Taos in New Mexico was built by Catholic missionaries in the early 1800s. It is one of the best known adobe buildings in the region.

Most kivas are underground, with a ladder leading down from an entrance in the roof. In Pueblo stories the first people climbed to the earth's surface from underground. Kivas symbolize the beginnings of the Pueblo people.

Pueblos often combine their traditional religion with the Catholic faith. They go to church as well as practice ancient Pueblo ceremonies. Pueblo dances often take place on days on which a Catholic saint is honored. Sometimes the Pueblos bring out the saint's statue from the church for the dance.

4 · A CHANGING WORLD

Less than a hundred years ago, experts predicted that the Pueblos would lose their unique culture and blend in with the rest of America. They were wrong. Today, Pueblo people preserve their religion and identity while living in the modern world.

Protecting their heritage is not always easy. Sometimes the Pueblos have to fight to preserve their holy places. In 1970 the people of Taos Pueblo won a long legal battle for control of their sacred Blue Lake. The Zunis saved Salt Woman Lake from a strip-mining project after a twenty-year-long struggle.

The Pueblos are also working to preserve their traditional languages. Seven of the New Mexican pueblos speak a language called Keresan. Six pueblos speak

A Pueblo grandmother smiles at her granddaughter at San Juan Pueblo. The Pueblos believe that with age comes wisdom. The elderly are honored among the Pueblo people.

dialects of Tanoan called Tewa, Tiwa, and Towa. The Zuni people have their own language, while most Hopi pueblos speak a language called Uto-Aztecan. Many Pueblo children speak English at home and learn their traditional language in school.

Taos Pueblo does not allow electricity or running water within its walls. Most members live in conventional homes outside the village, but return to the village for important ceremonies.

One way the Pueblo people protect their culture is through privacy. Years ago, the Spanish punished Pueblos for practicing their traditional religion. In the 1800s and early 1900s, the U.S. government also sought to ban Pueblo religious rituals. Fortunately, these attitudes are changing.

Santa Clara Pueblo children, in traditional costume, perform the Buffalo Dance.

The Tewa Language

Many Pueblo children learn their traditional language in school. If you were a child from one of the Tewa-speaking pueblos, you might learn words like these.

Pueblo word	Pronounced	English word
bee	bay	apple
pava	PAH-vah	bread
tse	tsay	dog
fo	foh	hair
pivi	PEE-vee	meat
to	toh	shirt

But because of this history, few Pueblos are willing to share details of their rituals with non-Pueblos. Visitors are usually welcome at public dances, but not at ceremonies inside kivas. Even at public dances, photography may be forbidden.

Pueblo children wait for their turn to participate in a Deer Dance.

The Pueblos are working for a better life by improving health care and education in their communities, protecting the environment, and helping their people get better-paying jobs. Water is also a source of concern. New Mexico and Arizona are dry lands and sometimes groups compete for the rights to use water. Together with the Navajo and other water users, Pueblos are seeking to protect water sources for future generations.

The poet and author Simon Ortiz was born in Albuquerque and raised at Acoma Pueblo.

A Zuni Indian makes turquoise and silver jewelry.

Pueblos today take good things from both worlds—the modern world of computers and videos and the age-old ways of their ancestors. Some, such as writers Leslie Marmon Silko and Simon Ortiz, have become famous far outside their communities. "Native people are part of American history, but our history is much older," says artist Cliff Fragua of Jemez Pueblo. "We still exist, and we will continue to exist. Our traditions and our culture are sacred to us."

· TIME LINE

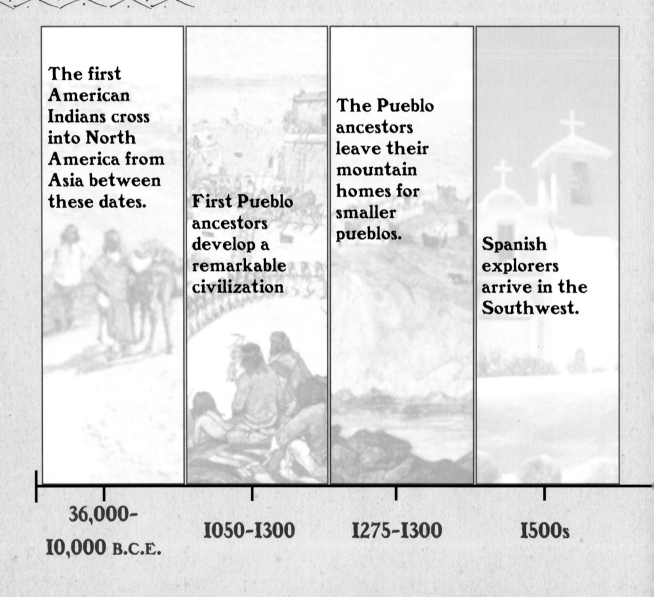

The first American Indians cross into North America from Asia between these dates.

First Pueblo ancestors develop a remarkable civilization

The Pueblo ancestors leave their mountain homes for smaller pueblos.

Spanish explorers arrive in the Southwest.

36,000–10,000 B.C.E.

1050–1300

1275–1300

1500s

The
Pueblos
revolt,
driving the
Spanish
from their
land.

The
Spanish
return and
gain control
once again.

Mexico
declares
independ-
ence from
Spain.

A treaty
with
Mexico
gives the
Southwest
to the
United
States.

Taos
Pueblo
regains
rights to
the sacred
Blue Lake.

I680   I692   I82I   I848   I970

· GLOSSARY

adobe: Clay mixed with sand or straw that is dried in the sun and used for building.

Anasazi: Early Pueblo Indian culture in the Southwest that lasted until about 1300 C.E.; a Navajo name meaning ancient enemies or ancient ones.

heritage: Something that is handed down from generation to generation; tradition.

kilt: A skirt that is worn by a boy or man when participating in a traditional ritual.

kiva: A room used for Pueblo religious ceremonies that is located underground.

manta: A traditional dress that covers one shoulder and is often worn over a shirt.

mesa: A flat-topped hill with steep sides.

metate: A flat grindstone made of stone used to grind cornmeal.

piki: A traditional Pueblo paper-thin bread that is baked on a hot stone.

pit house: An early Anasazi home in which the floor was dug several feet into the ground.

plaza: An open area in the middle of a pueblo where people gather for dances or other events.

pueblo: A village of stone or adobe houses where some southwestern American Indians live.

Pueblo Indians: American Indians who have traditionally lived in villages of stone or adobe.

ritual: A ceremonial act or action.

sacred: A thing or being that is worthy of religious devotion or worship; holy.

treaty: A formal agreement between two groups or nations.

turquoise: A type of blue-green stone used to make jewelry.

· FIND OUT MORE

Books

Arnold, Caroline. *The Ancient Cliff Dwellers of Mesa Verde*. New York: Clarion Books, 1992.

Bial, Raymond. *The Pueblo.* New York: Marshall Cavendish, 2000.

Hoyt-Goldsmith, Diane. *Pueblo Storyteller.* New York: Holiday House, 1991.

Hucko, Bruce. *Where There Is No Name for Art: The Art of Tewa Children.* Santa Fe, New Mexico: SAR Press, 1996.

Keegan, Marcia. *Pueblo Boys: Growing Up in Two Worlds.* New York: Cobblehill Press, 1996.

Noble, David Grant. *Ancient Indians of the Southwest.* Tucson, Arizona: Southwest Parks and Monuments Association, 1998.

Swentzell, Rina. *Children of Clay: A Family of Pueblo Potters.* Minneapolis: Lerner Publications Company, 1992.

Tomchek, Ann Heinrichs. *The Hopi.* Chicago: Children's Press, 1987.

Trimble, Stephen. *The Village of Blue Stone.* New York: Macmillan Publishing Company, 1990.

Yue, Charlotte and David Yue. *The Pueblo.* Boston: Houghton Mifflin Company, 1986.

Web Sites

Anasazi Heritage Center

www.co.blm.gov/ahc/hmepge.htm

Hopi Cultural Preservation Office

www.nau.edu/~hcpo-p/

Indian Pueblo Cultural Center

www.indianpueblo.org/

About the Author

Marian Broida has written seven books in the Marshall Cavendish Benchmark series Hands-On History, two of which are about American Indians. In addition to children's nonfiction books, Ms. Broida writes books for adults on health care topics and occasionally works as a nurse. She lives in Decatur, Georgia.